20 Popular Tourist Destinations in Penang, Malaysia

Hilmy Hamid

Contents

Introduction

The Penang State is hit as a holiday destination that is familiar to foreign tourists to pursue various & unique local foods. Signature food menu in Penang such as Laksa Penang, Nasi Kandar, Pupuk, or Mee Sotong are available. Foods are a must try for you to go anywhere in Penang. Interesting tourist attractions in Penang are just as great if not better than in other states in Malaysia, either at resort beaches, historic destinations, museums, outdoor adventures and friendly petting gardens for children.

So, let's review all the destinations of interest that are popular in Penang including the best locations for your activities. If you want to have a honeymoon in Penang, there are several locations that can provide you with charming resorts and hotels for your stay with your partner.

1 Penang Ferry

The oldest ferry service in Malaysia and a holiday experience in Penang. It is worth a ferry ride from the mainland to Pulau Pinang. One of the activities that kids will love and is very affordable. Travel from Butterworth to Penang island and back from the Island to Butterworth. The return trip is a free ferry ride.

Sultan Abdul Halim Ferry Terminal, 12000 Butterworth, Penang

<u>Penang Ferry Operation Time</u>

From Butterworth to George Town
1. First ferries: starts at 5.20 am
2. Last ferry: ends at 12.10 am

From George Town (on the island) to Butterworth

3. First ferries: starts at 5.40 am
4. Last ferry: ends at 12.40 am

The duration of each ferry trip is about 20-30 minutes.
The ferry walkway in Penang takes about 15-20 minutes

<u>Penang Ferry Ticket Prices</u>

Ticket fares are only payable one way from Butterworth to the Pulau Pinang section. From the Pulau Pinang to Butterworth, the trip is free.

Without a Vehicle (Pedestrians)
5. Adult (fare): RM 1.20
6. Children (5-12 years old): RM 0.60

Vehicles
Bicycles: RM 1.40
Motorcycles : RM 2.00
Car: RM 7.70

2. Fort Cornwallis

This Old Fortress is located next to Padang Kota Lama and is a pretty historical destination in Penang where this location was the site of Sir Francis Light's landing in 1876. The fort is still in good condition and the brick walls in the area are still intact and standing up. Inside the fort there are several buildings that are part of this fortress's function once before as a gun powder store, army camp, cannon, Old church and lighthouse.

Jalan Tun Syed Sheh Barakbah, George Town, 10200 George Town, Penang

Fort Cornwallis Penang Operation Hour
9 am - 10 pm (daily)

Fort Cornwallis Penang Ticket Prices

Mykad Holder
1. Adult: RM 10
2. Children: RM 5

Foreign Tourist
3. Adult: RM 20
4. Children: RM 10

Parking rates

5. RM 2 per first hour
6. RM 1 per next hour

3 Padang Kota Lama

An open-air seafront park which houses a well-equipped Public facilities both children's playgrounds, restaurants, toilets and others. It is often the location for community events like food parties and so on. The location is next to the Cornwallis Fortress and is an ideal place to relax in the evening and feel the strong breeze from the sea.

1, Light St, Georgetown, 10450 George Town, Penang

Operation Hours • 24 hours
Ticket Prices • free

4 Gurney Drive (Persiaran Gurney)

The destination is a popular beachfront lounging and eateries in Georgetown. The food stalls here mostly provide Penang's popular food such as spice curry, rojak and other local meals. The evening ambience is lively with hawkers and visitors who are taking in the night seafront breeze.

Gurney Drive, Georgetown, 10250 George Town, Penang

Operation Hours • 24 hours
Ticket Price   • none

5 Penang Street Art

3D paintings in Outdoors in JaLan Seni Penang, which makes this place unobtrusive, is an area with Old Buildings. Often become a tourist destination with a pic of sambiL walking around looking for food in the surrounding area.

316, Beach St, Georgetown, 10300 George Town, Penang

Operation Hour • 24 hours
Ticket Prices • none

6 Kapitan Keling Mosque

An iconic mosque in Penang that has been here since 1801. The building's architecture has the influence of Roman and Middle Eastern culture. This mosque was built to accommodate the increasing number of muslims, especially Indian Muslims. The location is just besides the restaurant of Nasi Kandar Beratur. After visiting this mosque, you can queue at this nasi kandar restaurant which is said to be among the most popular in Penang.

14, Buckingham Road, George Town, 10200 George Town, Penang

Operation Hours of Kapitan Keling Mosque • 24 hours
Ticket Prices Kapitan Keling Mosque • Faith &
                                  • Sincere donation to the mosque fund

7 Chowrasta Bazaar

This bazaar is a market that houses both wet and dry markets. Due to its strategic location in the city of Geoorge Town and easily accessible to the public, it is always filled with visitors to find fresh food stuff. In addition, there are also sections that contain various types of fruits such as oranges and bananas. On the second floor it is used to for dry items that includes books, shirts, accessories and others.

Lebuh Tamil, George Town, 10100 George Town, PuLau Pinang

Operation Hours Chow Rasta Bazaar
• 6.30 am - 6.00 pm

8 State Stadium Morning Market

Located at Jalan Stadium, this morning market is like Memory Lane in Perak. There are stalls and hawkers who serve food and sells other physical items. These include cd, wallets, Old novels, Old shoes, antiques and so on. Some local people call this place as a Rusted Market and some call it the Road Walk. For those who like to look for antique & rare items, you can do lots of shopping here. Mind you, antiques are not necessarily cheap!

JaLan Stadium, 10460 George Town, Penang BeLakang Stadium Negeri PuLau Pinang

Road Operation Hours • 6 am -1 pm

9 P Ramlee House

Here is where a great artist who works in the art industry around 50-70 years ago was born on March 22, 1929. This Old House, which is nipah & wooded, still maintains its architecture and home-like decor. As soon as you enter the house, with the accompaniment of P. RamLee's songs, you will see a lot of information about his personal life & career.

Lot 2180, JaLan P. RamLee, Kampar Park, 10460 George Town, PuLau Pinang

P. RamLee Penang Home Operation Hour • 9 am - 5.30 pm
Ticket Price • Free

10 Bukit Bendera

If you did not go to Bukit Bendera you would not be vacationing in Penang. For those who enjoy relaxing activities such as looking at beautiful sceneries, you can take the kids to the Bukit Bendera (Flag Hill) and take the train to the top. At the peak of Bukit Bendera, there are many interesting relaxing activities. The trip on the train to the top of Bukit Bendera is exciting even more so on the way down. If you want a greater sense of thrill, get a seat at the front of the cable car.

Bukit Bendera, George Town, Penang

Operation Hours

1. The train at Bukit Bendera operates daily and the itinerary starts as early as 6.30am to 11pm (the last train from the summit).

Tickets for Malaysian Citizens (MyKad holders):

2. Adult: RM 10 / pax (two way)
3. Senior Citizens> 60 years: RM5 / pax
4. Students: RM 5 / pax
5. Children (4-6 years old): RM3 / pax
6. OKU/Disabled: Free

7. FastLane Rate

8. Adult: RM 30 / pax (two way)
9. Senior Citizens> 60 years: RM5 / pax
10. Students: RM 15 / pax
11. Children (4-6 years old): RM3 / pax
12. OKU/Disabled: Free

Tickets for the Bukit Bendera Cable Car Ticket for none MyKad holders:

13. NormaL Rate
14. Adult: RM 30 / pax (two way)
15. Senior Citizens> 60 years: RM30 / pax
16. Students: RM 15 / pax
17. Children (4-6 years old): RMs / pax
18. OKU/Disabled: Free

19. FastLane Rate

20. Adult: RM 60 / pax (two way)
21. Senior Citizens> 60 years: RM60 / pax
22. Students: RM 45 / pax
23. Children (4-6 years old): RM5 / pax
24. OKU/Disabled: Free

Parking fee is RM5 per entry

11 Kek Lok Si Temple

A temple in Georgetown which is a tourist spot to see the uniqueness of Buddhist places of worship. The temple is very high and at the top visitors can see some statues of buddha and pagoda. The views of Georgetown from the summit are very interesting.

1000-L, Ria Valley Level 1,11500 Ayer Itam, PuLau Pinang

Operation Hour of Kek Lok Si Temple
• 7 am - 9 pm (daily)

Kek Lok Si Temple tickets

27. Free entry
28. Elevator : RM 3
29. Pagoda building entrance: RM 2

12 Penang Botanical Garden

A local recreation area for jogging / walking in the morning and evening. The Penang Botanical Garden is located at the bottom of the Penang Hill foothills. The garden landscape is also very peaceful with a variety of shrubs and cooling to the eyes. The park is also synonymous with the name Monkey Park with the locals because it has a lot of monkeys wandering around in the garden.

673A, Jalan Kebun Bunga, Pulau Tikus, 10350 George Town, Penang

Penang Botanical Garden Operation Hours • 5 am - 8 pm
Entry • free

13 Tanjung Bungah Beach

The beach destination is the lesser bustling side of Pulau Pinang and we can find here a fairly spacious beach area, ideal for an afternoon stroll to see the sunset. The bathing activities here is not available because there are jellyfish present. Nearby there is a resort that has an ideal beach as the accommodation destination when honeymooning in Penang. Near Tanjung Bungah Beach there is also a mosque that looks as if it is floating in the water especially during high tides.

Tanjung Bungah Beach, 11200, Penang

Open - 24 hours

l4 Batu Feringgi Beach

It is the most popular resort beach in PuLau Pinang and here there are various water sports activities that can be done such as parasailing, jetski, banana boating and so on. The beach is always full of tourists for bathing and recreation. The choice of accommodation for both resorts or hotels is also great here & around the beach is also a great choice of restaurants or shops selling popular Penang food.

Batu Feringghi Beach, 11050, Penang

0pen 24 hours - Depending on the activity

15 Batu Feringgi Night Market

A night market that sells various souvenirs such as keychains, clothes, handicrafts and so on. Located in Batu Feringgi and not far from Tanjung Bungah Beach. An attractive place in Penang for shopping souvenirs while having dinner here.

JaLan Pantai Batu, Batu Pantai Park, 11200 Tanjong Bungah, PuLau Pinang

Batu Feringgi Night Market Operation Hours
• 7 pm -12 am (daily)

16 Pulau Pinang National Park

Located at Telok Bahang and is suitable as a holiday destination for those who like activities like jungle tekking, camping, swimming and observing life in the jungle. There is also a canopy walkway and the most interesting thing is at Lake Meromiktik, a meeting area between freshwater lakes and the salty seawater. In this area there is also a very high water dam and has stunning waterfall views.

P. Pinang National Park Office, Jalan Hassan Abbas, Balik Pulau, Penang, 11050 Penang, Penang

Penang State Park Operation Time   • 7.30 am - 6.00 pm (daily)

Penang National Park Ticket Prices
1. Entrance fee to Penang National Park: Free

3. Payment across a canopy bridge in Penang National Park:
4. Adult: RM 5.00
5. Children: RM 3.00

17 Penang Butterfly Farm by Entopia

Penang Butterfly Park is now known as Entopia after the completion of the facilities upgrade in 2016. This butterfly farm houses a variety of unique moths and insects for viewing. The garden landscape is very beautiful and as soon as one enters, the garden will definitely make the kids happy seeing hundreds of butterflies fly freely over their heads. There are lots of interesting infographics & videos about the butterfly's life cycle that are very useful for enhancing children's knowledge.

830 JALAN TELUK BAHANG, 11050 PULAU

Penang Butter Farm Operation Hours by Entopia

Open daily: (including public holidays & weekends)   • 9:00 am - 7:00 pm

Last ticket sales & last enrty time - 5:30 pm.

Ticket Price Penang by Entopia

MyKad / MyKid price
6. Adult (13-59 years old): RM 49.00
7. Children (4-12 years old): RM 29.00
8. Senior Citizens (60 years & above): RM 29.00
9. FamiLy Package (2 adults + 2 children): RM 127

Normal price
10. Adult (13-59 years old): RM 65.00
11. Children (4-12 years old): RM 45.00
12. Senior Citizens (60 years & above): RM 45.00

13. FamiLy Package (2 adults + 2 children): RM 175

Ticket prices are cheaper by making reservations & also during promotional times.

Please contact - Learning@entopia.com

18 Tropical Spice Garden

A garden with a variety of tropical exotic plants in over 8 acres and over 500 plant species planted. Visitors can recognize herbal plants that are strangely shaped by its name. There may be some herbs here where you have heard before but have never known what their stems & leaves look like. There is also a cooking room and a shop to buy herbs and souvenirs.

Lot 595 Mukim 2, Jalan Teluk Bahang, Teluk Bahang, 11050 George Town, Penang

Tropical Spice Garden Penang Time Operation • 9am - 6pm daily
              • Last enrty at 5.15 pm

Tropical Spice Garden Penang Ticket Prices

Garden Audio Tour:
• Adult: RM 29.00
• Children (4-12 years old): RM 17
• Children (under 4 years): Free
• Elderly (60 years & above): 23
• Students (with student card): RM 12

Live Guided Tours (9am / 11 am / 1.30pm)
• Adult: RM 49.00
• Children (4-12 years old): RM 25
• Children (under 4 years): Free
• Elderly (60 years & above): 39
• Students (with student card): RM 39

19 Tropical Fruit Farm Penang

A fruit plantation that houses a variety of tropical fruit trees. The best time to come during the fruiting season and visitors enjoy the fresh fruits quoted directly from the Farm. This fruit garden tour package is provided by the owner at a reasonable price including a package of fruit and fresh fruit juices.

Jalan Teluk Bahang, 11000 Penang

<u>Tropical Fruit Farm Penang Operation Hours</u>

Lunches Buffet starts from 12pm - 3pm.

Guided Farm Tour (including Fruit Plate & Fruit Juice / BoLeh Walk-In) • 9am - 5pm daily

Lunch Buffet (reservation required / Minimum 20 people) • 12 pm - 3 pm

Dinner Buffet (requires booking / Minimum 30 people) • 6 pm - 9 pm

Guided Farm Tour (including Fruit Plate & Fruit Juice / Walk-In welcome)

1. Adult: RM 40

2. Children (5-12 years old): RM 30

Fruit Tasting

3. Normal: RM 10 / RM 13 per plate

4. Medium: RM 20 / RM 25 per plate

5. Large: RM 30 / RM 40 per plate

Lunch Buffet (reservation required / Minimum 20 people. / 12 pm-3 pm)

6. Adult: RM 35

7. Children: RM 25

Dinner Buffet (booking required / Minimum of 30 people. / 6 pm- 9 pm)

8. Adult: RM 60

9. Children: RM 50

20 Penang Bird Park

Located in the Butterworth area, this bird park is divided into two different zones: caged zone & open zone. An open zone exists where docile species are freely released and visitors can actively interact without borders. The caged zone places the more aggressive bird species.

Taman Burung Seberang Jaya, Jalan Todak, Seberang Jaya, 13700, Perai, PuLau Pinang

<u>Penang Bird Park Operation Hours</u>

Open daily: 9.00am - 7.00pm including weekends & all Public Holidays.

Ticket Prices Penang Bird Park

20. Adult: RM 38
21. Adult (MyKad): RM 23
22. Children-Fun (12 children): RM 20
23. Children (12+ MyKid): RM 13
24. Students (with uniforms): RM 10
25. Camera: RM 1
26. Video Camera: RM 5
27. OKU (OKU card): FREE

Hopefully the list of places of interest in Penang above will give you some ideas of the ideal destination suited to your personal interests. Plan your trip by buying tickets & finding accommodations at strategic locations for easy mobility. It was quite limited that George Town City was part of the holiday season, which sometimes made us feel happy for a while in Penang.

If on vacation in Penang, trying out the popular food is a must. Nasi Kandar is probably the most popular dish in Pulau Pinang which almost everyone likes. There are actually many interesting places to eat at in Penang, whether it is local or western food.

A view of Penang